The Legend of Roberto Cofresí
A Puerto Rican Hero

Written By: Janet Balletta
Illustrated By: Estella Mejia

The Legend of Roberto Cofresí ~ A Puerto Rican Hero
©2015 by Janet Balletta

All rights reserved. No part of this publication may be reproduced, stored in a retrieval system or transmitted in any form by any means electronic, mechanical, photocopying, recording or otherwise, except brief extracts for the purpose of reviews, without the permission of the publisher and copyright owner.

Cover Design by Estella Mejía

WRB Publishing
Palm City, FL 34990
wrb1174@gmail.com

ISBN-13: 978-0-9909040-2-1

Dedication

For Joseph, Jacob, Julian, and Elijah,
who wanted to explore the world of pirates
and corsairs.

Captains Jacob and Joseph lived with their family in the Sunshine State of Florida. They spent hours playing in their backyard pretending to be corsairs, sailing away on magical adventures, and searching for invisible treasure. It all started when their dad read them the story of Roberto Cofresí, the strongest and bravest corsair of all time.

Jacob and Joseph's dad worked the night shift and got home in the wee hours of the morning. He always tiptoed into their bedroom and kissed them on their foreheads. Usually, the boys were fast asleep, but Joseph, who was older, usually woke up.

"Dad, please read me a bedtime story," Joseph begged.

"Very well, I will read you the story of Roberto Cofresí, a famous corsair from Puerto Rico," his dad said.

"What's a corsair?" asked Joseph.

"A corsair was a person hired by the King to fight enemy ships," said his dad.

Long ago, Puerto Rico was ruled by Spain and the King of Spain hired corsairs to defend it. They fought pirate ships and then returned home with the treasure to split it with the King. Corsairs worked for the King; pirates did not work for the King. Anyone caught pirating was sent to jail.

"Why were pirates sent to jail?" asked Joseph.

"They were sent to jail for attacking and robbing other ships," said dad.

Roberto Cofresí was born in Cabo Rojo, Puerto Rico. As a young boy, he spent his time playing in the marina, watching the sailors navigate their ships in and out of port. He wanted to become a sailor when he got older. His father thought it was a crazy idea, but that did not stop Roberto of dreaming about sailing around the world.

"Why did his father think it was a crazy idea?" asked Joseph.

"Sailors had a bad reputation back then," his dad replied.

Later on, there was a famine in Puerto Rico and people did not have enough food to eat. By now, Roberto had become a skilled, young fisherman and was able to provide food for his family and friends. He was an expert at navigating ships and wanted to build a boat of his own. He worked day and night to build his first boat. It was named the Mosquito. He used the Mosquito to begin his work as a merchant sailor.

"Why did he name his boat after a fly?" Joseph asked his dad.

"It was a tradition in those days to name boats after harmless creatures," his dad replied.

Legend claims, the King hired Cofresí to defend Puerto Rico. A large crew of men joined Cofresí on the mission as they set out to protect Puerto Rico. Cofresí met people from many different countries on the ships he defeated. Legend says Cofresí became good friends with a man from Africa who joined his crew. The African matey cast a magical spell upon the ship, making it invisible to the enemy. This kept them safely hidden at night.

"What does mission mean?" asked Joseph.

"It means an important job or assignment," his dad said.

Whenever Cofresí found women and children on the ships he set them free and took them to smaller islands where they had a better chance of surviving. He was known as a man of chivalry because of the compassion he showed towards women and children.

"What does chivalry mean," asked Joseph.

"It means you are polite and courteous to women and children," explained his dad.

During the time of famine, the people of Puerto Rico loved Cofresí because of his generosity towards them. In return, they protected Cofresí from the authorities, which searched for him, by sending light signals to warn of nearby danger.

"Why were they searching for him?" Joseph asked his dad.

"The King heard Cofresí had gathered great treasure and wanted him captured so he could keep all the treasure for himself," his dad said.

Cofresí and his crew conquered over one hundred ships and treasures during his time as a corsair. People say he buried his treasure inside caves of Puerto Rico and Santo Domingo. Legend says no one can ever find the buried treasure because his African friend also put an invisible spell on the buried treasure. Countless men have gone mad in search of the invisible treasure.

"Did they have a map to look for the invisible treasure?" asked Joseph.

"Oh, yes. They had maps marking the places they believed the invisible treasure was buried," said his dad.

Some people say Roberto believed there was a beautiful mermaid, who guarded his ship at night. He said the mermaid serenaded him to sleep after a long day of fighting. Before retiring to sleep, Cofresí rewarded the mermaid for her protection by tossing jewels into the sea.

Suddenly, Jacob asked, "are mermaids real?"

"Sailors believe mermaids are real," explained his dad.

Eventually, the King became so desperate to capture Cofresí and claim his enormous treasure, that he offered a large reward. When people heard about it, they wanted to find him and turn him into the authorities to collect the reward money. Cofresí became the most "wanted man" of his time.

"What does it mean to be a wanted man?" asked Joseph.

"It means they search for a person until they are found," his dad replied.

One evening Cofresí was sailing his ship, the Ana, when a U.S. Naval Ship, the Grampus, attacked. The fighting lasted for a short while, as the Ana was no match for the giant naval ship. Cofresí and his crew were finally captured. They accused Cofresí and his crew of pirating, although, he was innocent of such crimes.

"What does accused mean?" asked Joseph.

"It means to be blamed for something," explained his dad.

Cofresí and his crew were sent to jail. His invisible treasure has never been found and people are still searching for it today. Roberto Cofresí is a Puerto Rican hero. His legend will live forever because of the kindness and generosity he showed to the people of Puerto Rico.

"What does generosity mean?" asked Joseph.

"It means to give or share with others," his dad replied.

"Dad, that's the best story you have ever told us," said Joseph.

Out of the blue, their mom burst into the room.

"Ahoy, Mateys! It's time for breakfast," said mom. "I see you have been up all morning telling pirate tales again," she said.

"I want to be a corsair like Roberto Cofresí!" yelled Joseph.

"Me too!" cried Jacob.

"You can sail the seas or go on an invisible treasure hunt all you want, but only after breakfast is finished," mom urged.

Eager to start their treasure hunt, Captains Jacob and Joseph bolted out of bed roaring, "Argh! Argh! Shiver me timbers!"

Teacher's Guide

Vocabulary:

1. Legend (noun): A traditional story about a famous person or thing.

2. Corsair (noun): A person hired by the King to fight enemy ships.

3. Famine (noun): A food shortage.

4. Pledge (noun): A promise or vow to someone or something.

5. Navigating (verb): Directing the course of a ship.

6. Generosity (noun): The quality of being kind and generous.

7. Reputation (noun): The beliefs held about a person.

8. Chivalry (noun): The quality of being polite and courteous towards women and children.

Questions:

1. Who was Roberto Cofresí?

2. Why is he called the Robin Hood of Puerto Rico?

3. What qualities did he have that make him a hero?

4. Who helped him escape the authorities?

5. How did the light codes help Cofresí?

6. What kind of spell did his African friend put on the ship?

7. If you were Roberto Cofresí, what would you do differently?

8. What lesson or theme does this story teach us?

The Legend of the Colombian Mermaid

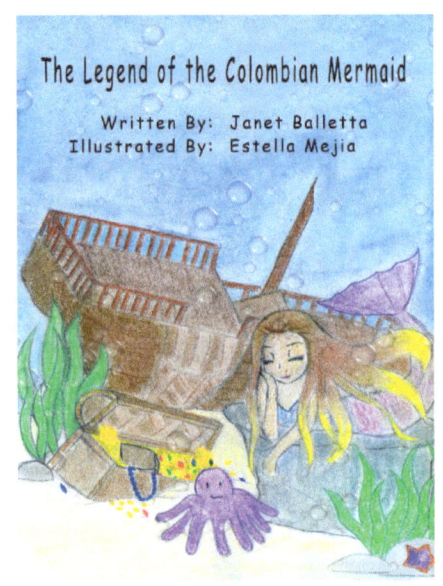

Janet Balletta is the author of "The Legend of the Colombian Mermaid" the story of a young girl who turned into a mermaid after she defied her parents and went swimming on Good Friday. In 2015, "The Legend of the Colombian Mermaid" won the Mariposa Award in the International Latino Book Awards. It was also nominated for 2015 Christian Literacy Awards. To learn more about this fascinating legend visit the website: Colombianmermaid.com. Her books are available on Amazon, Nook, and Kindle.

Amazon Reviews....

"This story shows children how the treasure of family is more important than the treasure of gold," says Carol Leonard.

"The Legend of the Colombian Mermaid not only tells a story with an important lesson but also incorporates important themes of religion and heritage. While this book is an excellent story to read during the holy Lenten season, it can certainly be enjoyed year round to celebrate a literary work with strong multi-cultural themes," says MW311.

"What an amazing story for both children and adults! This story brings you back to when you were a child. It is inspiring and such a lesson to be taught," says Lynn Psarris.

www.ingramcontent.com/pod-product-compliance
Lightning Source LLC
Chambersburg PA
CBHW042143290426
44110CB00002B/94